Unleash Your Inner CEO

The Country Girl's Guide to Being Your Own Boss

Dr. Linda R. Jordon

Published by
Hybrid Global Publishing
333 E 14th Street
#3C
New York, NY 10003

Manufactured in the United States of America, or in the United Kingdom when distributed elsewhere.

Jordon, Dr. Linda R.
Unleash Your Inner CEO
    ISBN: 978-1-957013-86-2
    eBook: 978-1-957013-87-9
    LCCN: 2023910567

Cover design by: Natasha Clawson
Copyediting by: Claudia Volkman
Interior design by: Suba Murugan
Author photo by: MediaExpertzy

www.lindajordon.com

Contents

Chapter 1   Be Yourself: You Have the Power to
             Make It Happen   1

Chapter 2   Be Strategic: Is It a Job or Is It a Career?
             Make a Plan and Create Your Strategy   9

Chapter 3   Be Self-Aware: No More Excuses!   19

Chapter 4   Be Mindful: The Importance of Self-Care   29

Chapter 5   Be Coachable: Confidant, Mentor, or Coach   39

Chapter 6   Be Curious to Learn: Invest in Yourself   49

Chapter 7   Be an Inclusive Leader: The Importance of
             Having a Diverse Culture   59

Chapter 8   Be an Engaged Leader: Don't Be
             That Crappy Boss!   69

Chapter 9   Be in Your Own Power: Know Your
             Boundaries and Live Life Intentionally   79

Chapter 10   Be Entrepreneurial: Have More Than
             One Plan B   87

CHAPTER 1

Be Yourself: You Have the Power to Make It Happen

Always Be YOU! When I was hired for my first real corporate job in 1989, I was excited, nervous, and anxious about working for a large company. You see, I had worked for smaller companies for many years and didn't feel nervous at all. But this particular company made me nervous as well as excited. This was going to be my first real job and I didn't want to blow it. I had worked hard to get this job and I wanted to be able to work there for thirty years, plus the job came with benefits and bonuses! Sometimes I would think I didn't qualify, and that it was a mistake. Did they really hire me? For some reason, I was very surprised that I was the top candidate for the job. I'm not sure why I doubted myself, but I did. Have you ever doubted yourself? Well, I did because I wasn't sure if I had the power to become a successful person. I was out of my element and didn't have a clue what to expect, but I will willing to give it a try.

I went into the interview, and I was relaxed. I bought a new outfit because I wanted to look professional and make a good first impression. During the interview, I started talking and let the manager know who I really was. I quickly made a connection with her, and she was very nice.

So, you are probably saying, who was I really? What does that mean? Well, the interview was great. We had a real conversation. Yes, there were a lot of questions, and I had to take a typing test, and a few other tests that I wasn't aware I'd have to take. Surprisingly, everything went great with the interview and the testing. During the interview, I talked about where I grew up, my previous work experience, and what I enjoyed doing in my spare time. I also shared that I wanted to excel in the position and what I wanted to achieve in my life. Although I was still nervous, I was acting like my normal, country-girl self, as we should all do every day.

Are there times when *you* feel like you can't be your authentic self? Are you hiding your true self at work?

Of course, there were times when I doubted myself and doubted my skills and capabilities. I even did extra work after hours because I lacked confidence. I needed to prove to myself that I could do it, and I wanted others to know I could fit in. We have all had self-doubt at some point in our lives. Most individuals have a lack of confidence regardless of how much experience or education they have. Today, the term most used for this is *imposter syndrome*.

You see, as I progressed up the corporate ladder, I wasn't always my true and authentic self. I thought I needed to be someone else to be successful and accepted. Unfortunately, I lacked the self-confidence to be the best to the point that I found myself playing a different role so that I could fit into a leadership role.

As a leader, you must show confidence in your abilities, speak with confidence when you deliver messages, and be able to influence others. Having self-confidence is even more important when you have a staff to manage. Your staff will look to you for guidance and support and if you show any signs of doubt, your employees may wonder what's going on. Your employees will start to lose confidence and trust in your abilities as a leader.

I often found myself questioning my own judgment because I got caught up in the corporate space. I wanted to be perfect, and I wanted to be the best leader. I was so focused on perfection and being the best that I lost my way at times. Yes, I lost who I was and most importantly, I felt like I lost my identity. I became that corporate leader who worked really hard, did everything right or perfectly, and followed the rules to the letter but still didn't feel like I was fulfilling my dream. It was really hard to be an African American female leader in the corporate space. I always felt like I had to do more and that more was expected from me.

Feeling like I had to do more as a leader often meant that I felt like I had to learn more than anyone, get as many certifications as possible, get more degrees, and always be on a project or assignment. There were many times when I was acting like the corporate queen. My husband would often say to me that my behavior at home was very different from my behavior at work. My husband also said that my voice changed when I would speak with him. He always knew when I'd had a bad day at work because he said my "corporate voice" would take over. Yes, I used the corporate lingo and my behavior changed as did the way I interacted with others.

When I needed to show more of my personal side to my team, I didn't. I was still the impersonal corporate leader. I couldn't shake myself away from trying to be perfect. Although I may have been a good leader, I felt like I wasn't a good person and that's a bad feeling.

For example, when I was faced with having to make business decisions about downsizing my department, I felt like I was doing something wrong. The leader in me followed the process that I was given; however, it didn't make me feel better about having to let employees go because the company was changing direction. You see, I had been through the downsizing, rightsizing, and layoff, process before, and each time I had to let people go whom I cared about. Unfortunately, some of my employees took it personally and felt like *I* was letting them go instead of the company. After going through this process so many times, my behavior started to change, and I was no longer being my authentic self. When my employees began to bring it to my attention, that's when I realized I needed to talk with a coach, and I also knew that I should have some type of self-assessment done.

I took a few leadership assessments such as StrengthFinders and DISC and was also assigned to a leadership coach. When I got my results, I was completely surprised. It was an eye-opening experience for me. At that moment, I realized that the assessments were very accurate based on my recent behavior and my communication style. Oddly enough, some of the findings related to my childhood and how I was raised on the farm. You see, bringing your authentic self to work also included letting people in on who I was as a person. The majority of the time at work, I didn't always do such a great job of letting people see the personal side of me. I was always taught to keep my personal life separate from my business life. I didn't always go out with colleagues after work unless it was a business meeting.

Often we as leaders get so caught up on productivity and the numbers at work that we forget the importance of doing a good job as a leader and being there for our staff. We also forget that our teams want to get to know us better and understand who we are on a personal level.

Well, that hit me hard one day at work during a large team meeting. It was getting close to the last day for some of the employees who were leaving as a result of the organizational change. I was at the podium speaking about their great work and how I would miss them when, suddenly, I felt the tears start to roll down my face, my voice start to quiver, and I couldn't stop shaking. I had held my feelings so close, and I had been so focused on work that I felt like I was about to explode. I sobbed while trying to speak, and that's when my team realized that I did have a heart and that I truly cared about them. After crying, I finished my presentation, but I was still shaking. As I stepped down from the stage, my team approached me with hugs and tears. We also got a good laugh out of it as everyone was surprised and pleased that I finally allowed myself to be human and be one of them.

I tried to keep my work life separate from my home life, and it didn't always work. That didn't come into play for me until my daughter was born. That's when I let my work family know more about me. My family was the most important and I had a husband and daughter to take care of. As a mom, my daughter had priority, so I needed to let others know more about who I was as a mom and as an individual. Yes, sometimes you must let your guard down and just be you.

Work life became easier when my daughter was enrolled in daycare on the company's campus. It was great because I could go see her during my lunch hour if time permitted. Once my staff began to learn about the personal side of my life, things started to change for the better. I was more relaxed as a leader, and I understood my staff's concerns from a different perspective. I know I became a better listener and a much better leader.

On December 4, 2014, I was working at my desk when my physician called and said she needed to see me right away. At once, I felt that something was wrong, and I knew it was going to be bad news. Two weeks before, I'd had a biopsy, and I was waiting for the results. I quickly left the office, unsure if I told my staff where I was going. I just knew I had to leave and hear what the doctor had to say.

As soon as I sat down in the doctor's office, I knew what my physician was going to say. I could tell she had bad news based on her behavior and body language. I don't remember anything after she said the words, "Mrs. Jordon, you have breast cancer." It was like I was in a daze. All I can remember is that I left the doctor's office and went home. I don't remember driving there. I do remember that I called my oldest sister on the way home. She had been diagnosed with breast cancer five years ago. I didn't call my husband immediately because I was a nervous wreck, and I know how my husband gets when he gets overly excited. I just needed to get home quickly.

I arrived home and my sister arrived forty-five minutes later, and then it was like a dream again. Before I knew it, my husband was home and most of my siblings had arrived. After a few moments of prayer and just absorbing the information, I knew what I needed to do. My husband and I discussed my medical options, and then I immediately scheduled my double mastectomy and reconstruction surgery with the physicians. The very next day, I opted for early retirement from my company. I had worked for this organization for over twenty-seven years, and I was hoping to make it to the thirty-year mark. However, life happened, and I needed to do what was best for me and my health. My surgery was scheduled and completed on February 12, 2015. Today, I am eight years cancer-free and doing great!

After surgery and healing, I knew I had to do something different with my life and I wanted to make a difference in the world. God had given me a second chance, so I needed to make the best of it, and I needed to start right away. I immediately knew that I wanted to leave a legacy for my daughter, and I wanted her to be proud of me.

So, on March 15, 2015, 30 days after surgery, I purchased a real estate franchise business with HomeVestors of America. My husband and I had already been purchasing rental properties for several years but it had not been a full-time enterprise. I had been involved in real estate as a side hustle and had been enjoying it. I knew that real estate was the best option for me to make a difference in the world while helping others in my community and at the same time building a family legacy.

Diamond Realty Investments, LLC was created on March 15, 2015. It's been eight years of full-time real estate investing; doing fix and flips, wholesaling and purchasing rental properties, and making new friends in the real estate investing business. As of today, we have over thirty rental income properties, and I would say that I am living my best life!

As I tell everyone, I was blessed with breast cancer. Having breast cancer made me realize that I needed to make a change in my life. Having cancer and being on medical leave allowed me the time I needed to take better care of my health, get off blood pressure medications, watch my cholesterol, and lose twenty pounds. Yes, it was my time and, yes, I had to do it then. How many of you are struggling with a decision to make about your business, your life, your health, or your financial situation? Don't overthink it. Overthinking will cause you to miss out on opportunities. It's your time and the time is NOW.

Dr. Linda's Kernels of Wisdom

Take a few moments to do this exercise:

Make a list of the three to five things that you want out of life. If you don't write them down, it's hard to hold yourself accountable.

_____

_____

_____

_____

_____

_____

Now, make a list of actions with specific timelines when you are going to make this happen.

_____

_____

_____

_____

_____

_____

Finally, take a few moments to write down how you will celebrate your success.

_____

_____

_____

_____

_____

_____

CHAPTER 2

Be Strategic: Is It a Job or Is It a Career? Make a Plan and Create Your Strategy

Which one would you prefer to have… a job or a career? A job is a paid position or occupation that an individual engages in to earn a living. It typically involves performing specific tasks and responsibilities within a particular industry or profession and can be full-time, part-time, temporary, or permanent. Different types of jobs require different levels of education, skills, and experience, and offer varying levels of compensation and benefits.

A career is a path or course of professional development that an individual chooses to follow, typically over an extended period. It involves mastering a particular set of skills, knowledge, and experience and may involve multiple different roles and positions within a particular industry or field. A career is often associated with long-term employment and the pursuit of personal and professional goals and aspirations.

One of the most critical mistakes leaders make is being indecisive. Too often leaders are hesitant and procrastinate when it comes to deciding on a project, a task, whether to hire someone,

9

whether to start a business, or just make a decision about anything. Leaders think they have all the time in the world to think about it, but they don't factor in the impact their decision has on others or themselves. I learned about the importance of decision-making and creating a plan from my parents. They taught me that if you fail to plan, you are planning to fail.

Growing up on the farm was a fun and exciting time in my life. Unfortunately, I didn't realize that until I became an adult. I remember my parents always telling my siblings and me, "Know what you want to do, stick to what you plan to do, and give it your all." My mom's favorite saying was, "If you are going to be a broom sweeper, be the best broom sweeper there is." At the time, I didn't know what that meant other than to keep the floors clean. As I reflect upon her words, I realize that I did what she said while I was working in the corporate space.

I took what my parents told me to heart. I lived by those words in life, but also in business. When I was a corporate leader, I was always very strategic. With every task I was given, I would establish the vision, create a strategic plan, and then work on that plan until it was implemented.

One of my corporate projects was designing, creating, and implementing a component of a contact center. This was an exciting task for me because I love process improvement. I was partnered with a fantastic HR professional named Kimberlee Spores. Kimberlee and I were excited to create change in the organization. One of the things I learned on this project was that once the leadership team made the decision, I was responsible for creating a plan to make it happen. The project plan was to be completed within two years or less, and we met the deadline. Along the way, I learned that I wasn't always flexible in my decision-making. Sometimes I would become too attached to a decision and couldn't think past it. As a leader, you need to be flexible in your thinking and able to adjust and make decisions in the moment. Business leaders who are strategic thinkers are more likely to make better decisions, they are more likely to achieve their goals, and they are more likely to be successful in their careers. Strategic thinking is important because it helps you to do four things:

1. Set goals that are achievable and realistic.

2. Identify the resources you need to achieve your goals.

3. Develop a plan to use your resources effectively.

4. Make decisions that will help you to achieve your goals.

Be Strategic: 8 Simple Steps

1. **Set a clear vision**: A strategic leader starts with a clear purpose and a well-defined set of outcomes. Identify what you want to accomplish and motivate your team by articulating a shared vision.

2. **Build a strong team**: No one person can achieve a large-scale strategy on their own. It's important to surround yourself with a strong team that can execute your vision. Hire people with complementary skills and experience and foster a culture of collaboration and shared success.

3. **Be data-driven**: To avoid making decisions based on gut instincts or assumptions, use data and analytics to inform your decisions. Regularly analyze metrics to assess your progress and make necessary adjustments.

4. **Focus on the big picture**: Strategic leaders stay focused on the long-term outcomes and how they can achieve them. Avoid getting bogged down in smaller, less impactful details, and stay focused on the overall plan.

5. **Create a culture of innovation**: Encourage creative thinking and experimentation to come up with new ideas and solutions. Provide your team with the resources and support they need to think outside the box and try new things.

6. **Maintain flexibility**: While having a clear vision is important, it's also crucial to stay flexible as circumstances change. Anticipate potential challenges and have contingency plans in place to pivot when necessary.

7. **Communicate effectively**: Communication is key to any successful strategy. Ensure that your team understands the vision, the plan for achieving it, and their roles and responsibilities. Provide regular updates and be open to feedback.

8. **Develop strong relationships**: Effective strategic leaders build strong relationships with their team members, stakeholders, and partners. Invest time and energy in cultivating these relationships to maximize success.

Just Do It!

As a leader, you have to be able to adjust to changes quickly. To be a successful business owner, you need to be able to make quick, intuitive decisions. Entrepreneurs have a unique cognition that provides them with the ability to identify, evaluate, and attain potential business opportunities. Through a thorough analysis of expertise, intellectual style, judgment, and conscious awareness, they can expedite the decision-making process. Research shows that leaders and entrepreneurs primarily used two methods to make decisions:

- **Rational decision-making**—based on logic without considering the emotional consequences of decisions

- **Intuitive decision-making**—based on unconscious ingenuity[1]

One of the secrets to being a good leader is making the decision and then taking action. Success comes when you can jump directly into the major to-do items and have the discipline to work on those items consistently until they're completed. In your action plan, create a timeline with each action item so you can finish the list on time. In other words, you can create your own project plan for efficiency.

When a leader makes a decision but doesn't take any action, it's a recipe for failure. We all make mistakes, but the important thing is to learn from your mistakes, so you don't repeat them again and again. When you have a decision to make, don't overthink it, don't procrastinate about it, just do it!

When Procrastination Strikes

Unfortunately, we are human so, yes, we do procrastinate and put things off. Procrastination is known as the act of delaying or postponing a task or action that needs to be completed, resulting in negative outcomes such as missed deadlines, increased stress, and lower productivity. People may procrastinate for various reasons, such as fear of failure, lack of motivation, distractions, or a tendency to prioritize short-term pleasure over long-term goals. Procrastination can become a chronic problem that affects various aspects of life, from academic and professional performance to personal relationships and well-being. Some strategies to overcome procrastination include setting clear goals, breaking tasks into smaller steps, eliminating distractions, creating a schedule or

---

1 Eling, K., Griffin, A., & Langerak, F. (2014), "Using Intuition in Fuzzy Front-End Decision-Making: A Conceptual Framework," *Journal of Product Innovation Management, 31*(5), 956-972.

deadline, seeking accountability and support, and practicing self-compassion.

- **Fear of failure:** Procrastination can occur when we are afraid of failing at a task or project. This fear can be so strong that we delay starting the project or task to avoid the possibility of failing.
- **Lack of motivation:** When we lack motivation, we may put off tasks or projects that require effort, thinking that we can do them later.
- **Perfectionism:** A desire for perfection can lead to procrastination as we wait for the "perfect" time or opportunity to begin a task or project.
- **Overwhelm:** When we are overwhelmed by the scope or complexity of a task or project, we may delay starting it or avoid it altogether.
- **Distractions:** We live in a world filled with distractions, both online and offline. These distractions can pull us away from our work and cause us to procrastinate.
- **Poor time management skills:** When we don't manage our time well, we may not have enough time to complete tasks or projects, which can lead to procrastination.
- **Lack of clear goals:** Without clear goals, it can be difficult to know what tasks or projects to focus on and when to do them, leading to procrastination.
- **Lack of accountability:** When we don't have anyone holding us accountable for our work, we may procrastinate more easily.

Although I have been successful in a variety of areas, I still sometimes find myself avoiding the tough decisions or doing the tough things. Yes, I still procrastinate in some ways. This is something that I think we all know we shouldn't put off doing but we still hesitate. As an entrepreneur, I often find myself delaying doing a Facebook Live. I do enjoy connecting with my audience but there are times when I am not sure if anyone is listening. When I get in that state of mind, I may tell myself that *It's okay to not show up today. Everyone is busy so they will watch the replay anyway.* OH NO!! Don't do it. Always show up every day. I learned the hard way that putting things off just makes it twice as hard. No matter how difficult it may be or how challenging it may feel, always show up for your viewers. Even if only one person is listening to your podcast or your FB Live. Show up anyway. You don't realize the impact you can have on one person.

Dr. Linda's Kernels of Wisdom

Taking action means that you are going to do something to make a change or achieve a goal. It involves making a conscious decision to move forward and actively work toward a desired outcome. Taking action requires courage and determination, and it often involves stepping out of your comfort zone. It can be as simple as making a phone call, sending an email, or having a difficult conversation, or it can be as complex as launching a new project or business. Regardless of the size or scope of the action, the most important aspect is that it is taken with purpose and intention.

It's just like when I was on the farm, and I was responsible for feeding the chickens. I had to get up early in the morning and get my chores done before the school bus arrived to drive me twenty miles to school. It wasn't my favorite thing to do, but I had to create a routine and get up on time to get everything done. Not only did I have to feed the chickens, but I also had to wash the dishes before I left home. One morning, I didn't wake up on time and I was late getting my work done. I found myself rushing and not completing the tasks correctly. It's 8:30 a.m. and I could see the school bus coming down the road. I grabbed my books and ran out of the house with the dish towel still in my hands because I had been in the middle of washing dishes. Unfortunately, I didn't make it, so I missed the bus that day. This taught me a lesson because my parents weren't going to drive me to school. I allowed distractions from the night before to interfere with my getting my homework done and going to bed on time. This resulted in me being inconsistent in my responsibilities and impacting my schooling. Lesson learned.

Three Steps to Taking Action

1. Be consistent in everything you do.

Being consistent can help build trust and credibility with your audience by demonstrating that you are dependable and committed to your beliefs. Consistency can also help you establish good habits, develop a strong work ethic, and achieve your goals by sticking to a plan and following through on your commitments.

Be consistent: Consistency is key when developing discipline. Commit to sticking to the routine even when it's difficult or inconvenient.

Learn from failures: Use failures as opportunities to learn and improve. Don't get discouraged if you slip up, just refocus and continue working toward the goal

2. Be disciplined and steadily work on your tasks.

Create a routine: Establish a consistent daily routine that incorporates all the necessary activities, such as exercise, work, and leisure.

Set goals and prioritize: Make a to-do list and set priorities for the day. Focus on completing the most important tasks first.

Eliminate distractions: Identify and eliminate anything that distracts from productivity, such as social media, games, or excessive TV.

Stay motivated: Find ways to stay motivated, such as rewarding oneself for accomplishments or visualizing the long-term benefits of being disciplined.

Practice self-control: Practice good self-control by avoiding impulsive decisions, sticking to a budget, and maintaining healthy habits.

3. Be committed and don't let the flying squirrels distract you from reaching your goals.

Be committed to having a strong dedication and willingness to see it through, despite any challenges or obstacles that may arise. It involves putting in the necessary effort and time to reach the desired outcome and having a steadfast determination to not give up or quit. Being committed also involves making sacrifices and prioritizing the task or goal at hand to make progress toward it.

Dr. Linda's Kernels of Wisdom

Now that you know the three steps to taking action, list three things on your to-do list that you have been putting off. Beside each item, list your next action step and a timeline for its completion. You are on your way to taking action and becoming your own boss!

1. _____

_____

_____

_____

_____

_____

_____

_____

Complete by: _____

2. _____

_____

_____

_____

_____

_____

_____

_____

_____

Complete by: _____

3. _____

_____

_____

_____

_____

_____

_____

_____

_____

Complete by: _____

CHAPTER 3

Be Self-Aware: No More Excuses!

Growing up, I struggled with understanding and dealing with my emotions. Happy, sad, angry, confused, and excited are emotions that we all deal with, but we don't always know how to manage them. Self-awareness is defined as being able to identify the way he or she feels about something. A person who can self-identify their strengths and weakness as well as be mindful of the impact they have on others is aware of their inner thoughts and reactions. As a leader, I was always mindful of the impact I have on my team and others around me. When I worked in the corporate office, my staff would tell me that they were unable to predict how I was going to respond to a crisis because I didn't show my emotions and always appeared to be calm.

The following example is based on a personal experience in which I utilized my self-awareness and relationship-building skills. At a former employer, there was a major crisis, and my team was frantic about a major systems issue. Systems were down and they were struggling with how to handle the situation. When they came to me, I listened to the problem and then asked the team how they planned to respond. They seemed surprised as if they were expecting me to become as excited and frantic as they were. However, I analyzed the issue as it was brought to me and asked the team for their suggestions. There were a lot of great suggestions, but the outcome would be based on which path the team decided to take.

My philosophy has been and continues to be to not take on the emotions of others because it will impact the rest of the team. My objective, in this case, was to keep the team calm and help them manage the situation, as they were all capable of coming up with a solution. After mulling it over, the team was confident in their ability to address the systems situation by involving the appropriate stakeholders and obtaining the appropriate resources needed to assist them. The team only needed me as a sounding board to bounce their ideas off of. My primary role was to coach the team through this crisis and encourage them to have confidence in their abilities.

The Importance of Self-Awareness as a Leader

Self-awareness is being able to identify the way you feel. When a person can identify their strengths and weakness as well as be mindful of the impact they have on others, they are aware of their inner thoughts and reactions. As a leader, you should be constantly mindful of the impact you have on your team and others around you. If your staff tells you they are unable to predict how you are going to respond to a crisis because you are reluctant to show emotions, this should raise a red flag for you. Staff want to feel they can come to their leaders; they want to feel and know they are in a safe space. So, it's OK for you as a leader to show emotions. It just lets your staff know you are human too and that you care. When you don't show emotions and are not transparent, there is an impact on the staff, which results in a change in the team atmosphere.

Emotional Intelligence Is a Critical Component of Effective Leadership Self-Management and Social Awareness

Self-management and social awareness are two components of emotional intelligence that are critical skills for leaders. When I was in corporate, one of the vice presidents in my organization did not possess the qualities of self-management or social awareness. She was capable of being optimistic when it came to opportunities that she was involved with, though, and she was very self-driven. Unfortunately, her behavior often came across to the team as negative. She had a high level of self-confidence; however, she lacked the business acumen to effectively communicate the business strategy to the team.

An example of this comes from one of my clients who shared during a recent meeting when she presented the vision and business strategy. The team had concerns about the vision statement as it wasn't inclusive of all departments within the organization. When team members expressed their concerns, she struggled with controlling her emotions during her response. Her response to the team was somewhat challenging as she struggled with why there was a level of importance to have a vision statement that was representative of all the teams. Unfortunately, the team felt demotivated and didn't think she was listening to them.

Relationship Management

The ability to influence others is a good quality of relationship management. Leaders can influence others and build powerful networks within and outside of their organization or network. This involves learning to first build strong relationships. From this foundation, you can more easily solve problems as they arise and move forward with what matters most. Establishing an alignment of interests with the group allows you to set the foundation of trust.

Be Fearless: Stop Making Excuses

Excuses are preventing you from living your best life.

There are three common excuses that we all use every day of the week.

Excuse #1 – We tell ourselves we don't have enough money.

Excuse #2 – We tell ourselves we don't have enough time.

Excuse #3 – We tell ourselves we don't know how.

Do you *really* want to be successful? If so, you need to stop making excuses for not getting the work done. The average person makes six excuses per day, which totals over 2,000 excuses per year.[2] We all make excuses for so many things. Oh, the lies we tell ourselves... I am too old, I am too fat, I am too skinny, I am not smart enough, I don't have enough education, I don't know enough people, no one will buy from me, and the list goes on and on! What if you told yourself enough excuses that you quit? For example, you didn't go to college because you didn't have enough money, or you didn't fire that bad employee because you didn't have enough time to do the paperwork.

The first step in overcoming your fear is to become aware of it and accept it. When you have the awareness of a fear, it puts you in control of that fear. The second step is to stop listening to the negative comments you say to yourself. Those negative comments are what keep those fears alive inside you.

---

2 Zoya Gervis, SWNS, "This Is How Many Excuses the Average American Makes Every Day," *New York Post*, May 18, 2020, https://nypost.com/2020/05/18/the-average-american-makes-this-many-excuses-every-day/.

The Three Most Common Fears

The three common fears that most people have are fear of failure, fear of rejection, and fear of not being good enough.

1. Fear #1: Failure

   No one wants to fail. We all want to be successful. You may have a fear of applying for that position you want or the promotion, trying to lose twenty pounds, or starting a business. The fear of letting yourself, your spouse, your parents, or your children down is what holds you back from moving forward. For me, the fear of failure popped up several times in life. When I was promoted years ago from a staff employee to a payroll supervisor, I was scared that I would let the team down. You see, the team and I were coworkers and became good friends. I wanted to do a good job but also wanted to make sure that I maintained my friendship with everyone. It is hard going from staff to supervisor while maintaining the leadership role. Although I had fear, I knew that through open communication, gaining respect from my team, and being a trustworthy leader, I would be successful.

2. Fear #2: Rejection

   I was the middle child of eight, and sometimes it was challenging for me to be seen and heard. When you are not the oldest or the youngest, it can be hard to fit in. Yes, I wanted the attention, and I wanted to be liked by everyone. I didn't realize the impact the fear of rejection had on me until I was an adult. I carried this feeling into high school, college, and into the board room. When I began working in the corporate space, I began to realize how the fear of rejection was impacting me as a leader of others. Most leaders want their staff to like them, so they end up doing a variety of 360 feedbacks or assessments.

3. Fear #3: Not Being Good Enough

So, who is going to listen to me? Oftentimes, that was what I was telling myself. I could hear the negative voices telling me I wasn't the smartest country girl, and I wasn't the prettiest. I often compared myself to others because I lacked confidence in myself. What made me think I could be successful in corporate America?

I overcame a lack of confidence by remembering what I learned on the farm. My parents always taught us to not compare ourselves to others. You see, on the farm, we didn't have a lot to do except work and go to church. So, my siblings and I started a singing group. As the youngest in the group, I was afraid to sing solo. I didn't want to mess up and forget the words. My oldest brother, James, was the leader of the group. He took time with me to help me overcome the fear and made me feel more confident in my abilities. He would always say, "Do your best, and God will take care of the rest." With lots of practice, I felt more confident in myself, and I was able to sing in front of the church with no fear. What I learned from that experience helped me overcome my fear as a leader in the corporate space. I learned that as a leader, I shouldn't compare myself to others because no one will lead the way that I would lead.

The Importance of Your Emotional IQ

Emotional intelligence refers to the ability to identify and manage one's own emotions as well as the emotions of others. It encompasses a range of skills, such as empathy, self-awareness, and emotional regulation.

Having emotional intelligence means being able to recognize and understand your own feelings and express them in a healthy and constructive way. It also means being able to interpret and respond to the emotions of others with sensitivity and compassion.

People with high emotional intelligence are often effective communicators, able to express themselves clearly and listen actively to others. They are also skilled at managing conflict and solving problems in a collaborative and respectful manner.

Perhaps most importantly, emotional intelligence is closely linked to resilience and mental health. When we can regulate our emotions and cope with stress effectively, we are more likely to feel satisfied and fulfilled in our personal and professional lives.

So how can we develop our emotional intelligence? It starts with self-awareness, or taking the time to reflect on our thoughts, feelings, and behaviors. We can also practice active listening, where we genuinely try to understand the perspective of others without judgment or defensiveness.

Other strategies include cultivating empathy, learning to manage stress and anxiety, and focusing on our strengths rather than dwelling on weaknesses. By investing time and energy in developing our emotional intelligence, we can become more resilient, compassionate, and effective human beings.

Being self-aware means that you have an understanding of your own personality, emotions, strengths, weaknesses, and motivations. When you are self-aware, you know what you want in life, and you are in control of your thoughts, feelings, and behaviors.

Self-awareness is not just about knowing who you are, but also about understanding how you are perceived by others. It involves being able to recognize your own biases, limitations, and blind spots as well as the impact of your actions on those around you.

Being self-aware requires a willingness to examine yourself objectively and identify areas where you can improve. It involves taking responsibility for your own strengths and weaknesses and working to develop your natural talents and abilities.

Self-awareness is essential for personal growth, emotional intelligence, and successful relationships. By acknowledging your own feelings and needs, you can better understand the needs and feelings of others. This enables you to communicate effectively, build trust, and establish meaningful connections with others.

In conclusion, being self-aware is a valuable skill that can help you navigate life's challenges with greater ease and grace. It requires ongoing self-reflection, introspection, and an open-minded approach to personal growth. By developing your self-awareness, you can become a more authentic, confident, and compassionate version of yourself.

The ability to influence others is a good quality of relationship management. Leaders can influence others and build powerful networks within and outside their organization or network.

One of the directors on my team did an excellent job in building relationships to gain buy-in and support when working on his business plans. He makes every attempt to align positive alliances with others to gain cooperation, overcome obstacles, and make progress on business objectives. The most important step he has identified in leading through an influence approach was recognizing its importance and encouraging his team. Establishing an alignment of interests with the group allowed me to set the foundation of trust.

Dr. Linda's Kernels of Wisdom

Don't let fear or excuses get in the way of your dreams and living your best life. Celebrate your wins daily and work hard on correcting your mistakes. Stop allowing fear, excuses, and limiting beliefs to take control.

Exercise:

Write down one limiting belief about yourself that you wish you did not have.

_____

_____

_____

Write down a belief that you want to have about yourself that is the opposite of your limiting belief.

Write down two ways in which you can handle your emotions.

#1 _____

_____

_____

_____

_____

#2 _____

_____

_____

_____

_____

CHAPTER 4

Be Mindful: The Importance of Self-Care

Now that you are the boss, you need to understand the importance of taking time for yourself.

I have been an entrepreneur for eight years, and I still find it challenging to schedule time for myself. We all get so busy with our daily activities that we often forget to take a break. A great example is when I am managing a fix-and-flip project. For those who may not know, fix and flip is purchasing a property, making modifications, and then reselling it on the market. Often I will schedule the contractors on-site and get them started on the work, schedule appointments with the cabinet department at Lowes, and run small errands to pick up items that the contractors may need. I will get so involved in the daily activities that I forget to do something as simple as take a lunch break. Although I am the boss, I still have to eat. If I don't eat on time, I find myself bingeing on snacks when I finally get home. But all it takes is a few minutes to stop and grab a bite to eat.

We all lead busy lives, and it's easy to get caught up in the hustle and bustle of our daily routines. However, it's important to take some time for ourselves to recharge and rejuvenate. Here are some ways to take time for yourself:

1. Create a quiet space: Carve out a quiet space in your home where you can relax and unwind. This could be a cozy corner with a comfortable chair, some candles, and your favorite book.

2. Exercise: Exercise is a great way to take time for yourself. Whether it's a morning jog, a yoga class, or a bike ride, getting some physical activity can help boost your mood and reduce stress.

3. Meditation: Meditation is a great way to calm your mind and focus on the present moment. Find a quiet spot and spend a few minutes each day meditating and breathing deeply.

4. Indulge in self-care: Take a relaxing bath, give yourself a manicure, or schedule a massage. Whatever makes you feel pampered and cared for, indulge in it.

5. Connect with nature: Spending time in nature can be incredibly rejuvenating. Take a walk in the woods, visit a nearby park, or plant some flowers in your garden.

Taking time for yourself doesn't have to be complicated or time-consuming. Just a few minutes each day can make a big difference in your overall well-being. So, take a deep breath, unwind, and prioritize your own needs.

Being mindful can be described as being aware and present in the moment, recognizing and acknowledging one's thoughts and feelings without judgment. It involves focusing on the present while letting go of distractions and past or future worries. Being mindful can help reduce stress and anxiety, improve emotional regulation, and enhance overall well-being.

To practice mindfulness, it's important to find time to fully engage in the present moment–whether that's through meditation, mindful breathing exercises, or simply taking a break to be still and observe one's surroundings. It's also crucial to embrace a nonjudgmental attitude toward oneself, recognizing that thoughts and feelings are natural and valid but do not necessarily define who one is as a person.

Relaxation

Relaxation is crucial for our physical and mental well-being. Here are some reasons why:

- Reduces stress: Relaxation helps in reducing stress levels by lowering the distribution of stress hormones such as cortisol and adrenaline in the body.
- Mental health: Relaxation encourages mental peace and lowers anxiety levels. It leads to increased self-esteem and a better attitude toward life.
- Physical health: Relaxation techniques that include meditation and deep breathing can help lower blood pressure and improve sleep.
- Better decision-making: With a relaxed mind, one can make better decisions as they are better able to evaluate the situation and weigh the pros and cons.
- Improved productivity: Relaxation can help improve concentration levels and enhance creativity. This leads to better productivity at work.

Overall, relaxation is essential for our physical and mental health, and it should be a vital part of our daily routine. Taking breaks, spending time with loved ones, indulging in hobbies, and practicing relaxation techniques can all help us relax and improve our well-being.

Exercise

Exercise is important for various reasons, including:

- Improves physical health: Regular exercise helps to improve heart and lung function, strengthen muscles and bones, lower blood pressure, improve balance and coordination, and reduce the risk of chronic diseases such as obesity, diabetes, and heart disease.
- Boosts mental health: Exercise is known to release endorphins, which are natural mood boosters and reduce stress levels. It also helps to improve cognitive function, memory, and mental alertness.
- Increases longevity: Studies have shown that individuals who exercise regularly tend to live longer than those who do not exercise. Exercise can help to reduce the risk of premature death from various causes.
- Promotes weight loss: Exercise can help to burn calories and lose weight. It also helps to increase metabolism, which can help maintain weight loss in the long term.
- Enhances overall quality of life: Regular exercise can improve overall physical and mental well-being. It helps to reduce feelings of anxiety and depression, improve self-esteem, and increase energy levels.

Overall, exercising is essential for maintaining a healthy and happy lifestyle. It is important to find an exercise routine that works for you and to make exercise a regular part of your daily routine.

Reading

Reading is another way to help you relax and reduce stress in your life. Here are a few simple tips on why taking time out of your busy schedule to read is important:

- Improves cognitive function: Reading stimulates the brain, improves memory and concentration, and helps develop critical thinking skills.
- Expands vocabulary: Reading introduces new words to the reader, which expands their vocabulary and improves their ability to communicate effectively.
- Enhances empathy: When readers engage with characters and their stories, they can develop a greater understanding of different perspectives and experiences, which can improve their empathy toward others.
- Provides relaxation and stress relief: Reading can be a form of stress relief and relaxation, allowing the reader to escape from reality and engage with a story.
- Increases knowledge: Reading provides access to vast amounts of information and knowledge, allowing readers to learn about new topics, cultures, and perspectives. In summary, reading is an essential life skill that improves cognitive function, expands vocabulary, enhances empathy, provides relaxation and stress relief, and increases knowledge.

Healthy Eating

Eating healthy is important for many reasons, including:

- Maintaining a healthy weight: Eating a balanced diet can help manage weight and prevent obesity, which in turn can reduce the risk of chronic diseases.
- Improving overall health: Eating a variety of nutrient-dense foods can provide essential vitamins, minerals, and nutrients that promote health and reduce the risk of chronic diseases like heart disease, diabetes, and some cancers.

- Boosting energy levels: Eating a balanced diet provides the body with the necessary fuel to perform daily activities and maintain energy levels throughout the day.
- Improving mood: Eating a balanced diet can help improve mood and reduce feelings of anxiety and depression.
- Enhancing cognitive function: Eating a balanced diet can improve brain function and protect against cognitive decline.
- Improving sleep quality: Eating a balanced diet can help regulate the sleep/wake cycle and promote better sleep quality.

Eating healthy is crucial for overall health and well-being and can help prevent chronic diseases while supporting a healthy weight and optimal body function.

My One-Hour Minute

How many times have you forgotten to do something because you were so busy with work? What was the impact on you or your health? As business owners, we feel we have to get everything done quickly because we are so busy making things happen. For me, I started doing what I call my "one-hour minute." It just means that I take one minute of the day to pause and reset myself. It seems like I took a one-hour break, but it really is just one minute.

When you find yourself stressed out, feeling like nothing is going right, or you are just exhausted, stop and take that one-hour minute to breathe and then restart. You will be amazed at the difference it can make. That extra burst of energy is all it takes to help you get through the rest of the day!

Here are ten practical tips that you need to incorporate into your one-hour minute of quality time for self-care.

1. Schedule fifteen minutes a day for thinking and focus time.

2. Take five minutes each day and say positive affirmations.

3. Go to lunch! Stop eating at your desk . . . it's not healthy.

4. Take a fifteen-minute walk and enjoy being outside.

5. Take fifteen minutes to read a good book.

6. Take a fifteen-minute nap.

7. Watch a funny movie or comedy. Laughter brings joy into your life.

8. Do breathing exercises.

9. Keep a journal–journaling is good for the soul.

10. Do some yoga or some stretching exercises.

Positive Affirmations

When you start to feel like you are overwhelmed and you don't have time to take a breath, take a few minutes, get out your journal, and write out the following "I will" affirmations. This is a simple task that will help you relax.

I will take time to have a healthy meal.

I will take time to focus on what I am doing before I make a decision.

I will not allow others to rush me.

I am confident and capable in all that I do.

I am deserving of love and respect from myself and others.

I trust in my own abilities to overcome any obstacle.

I am grateful for all that I have in my life.

I am worthy of success and happiness.

I choose to see the positive in all situations and find solutions.

I believe in my unique journey and trust the universe to guide me.

I am constantly improving and growing into my best self.

I am filled with strength, courage, and determination.

I radiate positivity and light to those around me.

Dr. Linda's Kernels of Wisdom

Write down three more of your own "I will" statements.

I will

_____

_____

_____

I will

_____

_____

_____

I will

_____

_____

_____

Here are a few examples of positive affirmations: Take a few moments and write down three affirmations that you will begin to use to help you get going.

I am grateful for what I have in life.

I am beautiful inside and out.

I love myself and everyone around me.

Continue to create affirming thoughts:

I am

_____

_____

_____

I am

_____

_____

_____

I am

_____

_____

_____

Now, write down three things that are constant impacts on your daily routine and decide that you will no longer allow these items to get you off track.

1. I will not allow _____

_____

_____

_____

2. I will not allow _____

_____

_____

_____

3. I will not allow _____

_____

_____

_____

CHAPTER 5

Be Coachable: Confidant, Mentor, or Coach

Most of you have heard a great deal about coaching, getting a coach, or being coachable. So, what does this all mean? Coaching is a process through which an individual helps another person or group to achieve their goals, develop their skills and knowledge, and improve their performance. It is a collaborative process that involves the coach asking questions, providing support and guidance, and encouraging the coachee to find their own solutions and strategies.

Coaching can be applied in many different areas of life, from personal development and career advancement to sports and business. It is often used by leaders and managers to help their team members improve their performance, by educators to assist students to learn and grow, and by therapists to support clients in overcoming challenges and achieving their desired outcomes.

Coaching is based on the belief that individuals can identify and achieve their goals on their own with guidance and support. The coach acts as a facilitator, helping the coachee to identify their strengths and weaknesses, set achievable goals, and create an action plan to achieve these goals.

Coaching is a powerful tool for personal and professional development, enabling individuals and teams to achieve their full potential and reach new heights of success. It fosters a culture of growth and learning and helps individuals build confidence, resilience, and self-awareness as they navigate life's challenges and pursue their dreams.

Coaching is all about you, the individual. If you are working with a coach, it is important to set aside dedicated time for your coaching sessions. You want to focus only on your coaching time with your coach, which means no phone calls, no checking emails, or anything else that would distract you.

When you are being coached, your objective is to share your goals, challenges, ask questions and share any obstacles that are preventing you from being successful. My three-step formula to reaching your goals while being coached is very simple: 1) Gain clarity on your goals; 2) Create options for achieving your goals and 3) Create an action plan to reach your goals.

Being honest and transparent with your coach is the key to having a good coaching conversation. As a coachee, you should ask yourself good questions and have the courage to open up and expand on your answers to include more details about your perspective and what you are thinking. If you are not willing to share with your coach, it will be difficult for your coach to help you.

Coaching is not the coach dictating to you. It's a collaborative process that pulls out the best within you. Coaching is not about you being silent… coaching is about sharing what you need help with. So, make sure you find a good coach to help you reach your goals.

Coaching has become a more popular business in recent years. Everyone needs coaching in some form or fashion. If you are looking for a good coach, I would recommend that you first understand the difference between coaching, counseling, and mentoring. Often, people think they are the same. If you are someone who wants to be told what to do, then I would suggest you look for a mentor.

If you are looking for someone to help guide you to greatness and help you fulfill your goals and objectives, then a coach is what you need. Here are the three types of coaching that you may come across when looking for a coach:

Confidant

From the time I was old enough to remember, I have always had someone in my life who has helped and guided me along the way. Studies have shown that people who succeed in life typically have a coach, a mentor, or someone they can talk to or a confidant. In my early years of adulthood, I had my older brother as a confidant. I could chat and tell him everything that was on my mind. He would share his perspective and provide me with excellent advice. As I started working in corporate America, I realized that having someone like my older brother was very important. At work, I needed someone to talk to about various issues or concerns I had, and I needed someone who would not have any judgment about the information I shared. Starting out, leadership didn't provide me with a coach. I sought out a mentor who could help me.

Mentor

So, what is a mentor? A mentor is someone whom you connect with, feel comfortable speaking with, and who has experience who can answer questions you might have about career advancement, business, or life in general. Having a mentor is great because that person will be open and honest with you when it comes to real-life examples. They will share their experiences with you, which will consist of the positive and negative things that have happened in their career.

Coach

Coaching is all about helping the individual and the organization and providing support to their needs. It is important to set aside dedicated time for each coaching client. You want to focus only on your client during this time . . . no phone calls, no checking emails, or anything else should distract you from your client.

A coach's objective is to do more listening and less talking. Coaching is designed to ensure that each individual has the right tools, guidance, and information to assist them in being able to have a clear and meaningful conversation and to have clear actions as part of their development process.

Asking good questions and listening is the key to having a good coaching conversation. Your coach should ask good questions to encourage you to open up and expand on your answers to include more details about your perspective and what you are thinking. Coaching is not telling the individual what to do or say. Coaching is not about asking closed-ended questions which do not allow the individual to express themselves. Coaching is not about you doing all of the talking . . . coaching is about listening.

A good coach's goal is to help the client solve the problem they bring forward during a session. My own process follows the following three-step formula: create clarity, generate options, and move to action.

1. **Create clarity**. I always start by asking the client how I can help them or what areas they would like to focus on. I then identify the issue or topic of discussion. During the conversation, I will ask, "What is the outcome you are looking for?"

2. **Generate options**. After the client has shared the topic and provided specifics about the issue, I ask them what other options they have to solve the problem. I also want to know if these options are possible and what obstacles they perceive

may come their way. I also will inquire about what resources they can utilize to assist in this process.

3. **Move to action**. During this step, I want the client to share their plans or actions they are going to take. I want them to provide details such as the timeframe for taking action. I also want the client to share what success will look like for them. It is helpful to the client to be able to visualize success, which always helps to motivate them to take action.

While working in corporate, I experienced similar difficulties that my clients faced. I started working in the corporate world in my early twenties. As a female of color, I always felt that I had to work harder and do more in order to be seen and heard. When I first started in corporate, I had not finished my undergraduate degree due to lack of funding. So, I found a job in hopes that this would help me pay off some bills and go back to college. Well, that didn't work out as planned so I kept working. I loved my job; the pay was OK at the time, but I wanted more.

Without a college education, I was limited in what I could do so I applied to NC Wesleyan and completed my bachelor's of science in business administration. I thought having a degree would surely get me over any hurdles I might encounter. Yes, having a degree was helpful to a point. When I wanted to progress in my career and move into leadership, I was faced with obstacles such as not having enough experience and not having a master's degree. So, here I go again . . . I applied for a master's of science in organizational change and leadership. This time, having a master's degree helped a great deal. I was able to move up in the organization; however, I still faced challenges.

Again, being the only person of color in leadership in my area was difficult at times. Balancing work and life while having a career can be demanding. Do you stay late for a meeting and miss picking up or child so that your spouse has to drive thirty minutes to get to daycare? Do you not attend a business dinner because your child has a ball game? You have to figure out what your priorities are.

I had additional challenges, too. I would receive feedback such as: I didn't talk enough in leadership meetings; I was too aggressive, or my feedback was not received well; I didn't show I cared; I didn't share more about myself and my personal life. At this point, I felt like it was a no-win situation. So, I asked for a coach and attended a variety of leadership training sessions. I wanted to fix whatever wasn't working.

My coach helped me see that I was a wound a little too tight because I wanted to be perfect as a leader, mom, and wife. I was trying to manage and juggle all three in hopes that I would be seen as someone who could handle a senior leadership role. After several years of coaching and then becoming a mentor to others, I realized the importance of always having a coach. Think about it this way: Every professional athlete has a coach–basketball, tennis, baseball, soccer, hockey, gymnastics, and skiing. Without a coach, my daughter would not have received a college scholarship for softball. My daughter started pitching when she was five years old. She wanted to play in college, so we hired a coach. Her coach helped her improve her craft and she learned a variety of pitching techniques. Although my daughter taught herself to pitch, having a coach made her even better. In life, you can become good at what you do. With a coach, you can become great at what you do.

How Do You Pick a Coach?

Picking a coach is a personal choice and can be a little scary if you have never done it before. Some of you may be fearful of being coached and that's OK. Fear is a state of mind. There is nothing to be fearful of when it comes to coaching if that is what you desire to do. We all do some form of coaching daily with our family and friends, although you may not realize it because you are having a conversation with them. And that is truly what coaching is all about... having a conversation with someone to support them in achieving their goals and dreams. So, let go of those fears and find the best coach and allow them to help you be your best because the world is waiting for you.

The first thing to do when selecting a coach is to interview the person you are considering as a coach. Ask them a variety of questions to determine their communication style, their values, who they've coached before, and what type of coaching style or program they are offering. If your values are different than the potential coach, then it may not be a good fit. If you are more of an introvert, you may need a coach who can match your style but also be able to push you a little. Remember, selecting the right coach can be life-changing; make sure you do your homework and pick the one that will serve you the best.

Elements of Coaching Models

Brief Solution-Focused Coaching	Constructive-Developmental Coaching	The Coaching Model
Future-focused	Asking good useful questions	Obtain agreement on goals
Creating a coaching environment of process for change	Good listening skills	Direct Observation
Ask catalytic questions	Obtaining feedback or getting an assessment of the person's skills	Prepare for the discussion
Having a strong trusting relationship	Establishing a good relationship	Giving and receiving feedback

Collecting feedback	Webs of belief	Follow-up meetings/sessions
Agreement on goals	Focused on development	Effective & active listening
Active listening	Conversation approach	Ask probing questions
Use scaling questions	Results-oriented	Gaining trust
Knowledge of internal resources	Be challenging and supportive	Creating a coaching environment

Common Elements

Although these are three different approaches to coaching, there are common elements in the models. Some of the common elements are active or effective listening, asking good questions, building a good relationship, and sharing feedback. The Coaching Model and Brief Solution-Focused Coaching are similar as they relates to gaining agreement on the goals and creating a good coaching environment.

Model Usage

The Constructive-Developmental Coaching model is best suited for coaching an individual dealing with change. When a leader is trying to coach an individual and provide a new way of looking at things, the better approach for coaching would be the Brief Solution-Focused Coaching model.

The Coaching Model is a four-step process: preparation, discussion, active coaching, and follow-up. This model is commonly used when a coach needs to have a good understanding of the person's behavior, skills and capabilities.

In reviewing all three models, the most effective one to use when coaching subordinates would be the Coaching Model. This model allows the coach to observe the individual and gain insights into their behavior and overall performance. Having insight into potential gaps and learning opportunities will aid the coach in the coaching discussion.

Coaching Is Not for Me!

Everyone would like to believe that they can solve their own problems. However, most of us cannot. When we try to solve our own problems, we start well and then we get distracted or become too personally attached to the situation. For example, I thought I could solve my problem of keeping up with social media posts, creating memes, and sending emails out daily. I quickly found out that it was impossible. I struggled with hiring someone to help me because I figured it was easy enough for me to do if I placed it on my calendar. I quickly found out that this made my problem even bigger. I was way farther behind than when I originally started. I just didn't have the time to focus on it daily. So, I decided to hire a virtual assistant.

When I hired someone to discuss the problems I was facing with social media and marketing and had them focus on the daily task, I felt a huge relief. I didn't realize how much time it took to get marketing done the right way. It also provided me with more time in my schedule to focus on the business and making money.

You might think you can tackle something better than someone else because you know it and understand it. Unfortunately, I am here to tell you that it doesn't work that way. We all need a coach, a mentor, or some other form of support to help us fix our problems. Doing things in a silo is not healthy and definitely not profitable.

Dr. Linda's Kernels of Wisdom

1. Learn more about the type of coach that will help serve you the best. So, do your research.

2. Attend workshops, seminars, or webinars from a variety of coaches so that you can gain an understanding of their coaching style, which will help you make the best choice.

3. Schedule a free consultation with a coach or mentor.

4. Write down what you are expecting from a coach and share it with them during your free consultation.

5. Select a coach. Don't overthink it. The more you think about why you need a coach, the less likely you are to hire a coach.

CHAPTER 6

Be Curious to Learn: Invest in Yourself

Since my early years as a teenager, I have always had the desire to want and do more. Probably because I was a middle child. Being a middle child, you don't always get what you want, you don't always have the attention of your parents because you're not the oldest or the youngest. So, I had to figure out how I could stand out in the crowd. For me, it was learning and being the best in hopes that I would get more attention. At home, this tactic didn't work, but in the workplace, I had the opportunity to learn as much as I could and would receive rewards for doing a good job.

When I first started in corporate, I wasn't sure about how much I needed to learn so I became curious about how to excel at my job, learn more about how the company operated, how the company generated revenue, and how employees got promoted.

Most employees want to do a good job. I wanted to excel at my job and get to the next level. So, yes, I learned my job really well and then quickly began to learn more about the department I was working in. I took the time to learn each person's role and connected with other departments to ensure that we were meeting expectations. By this time, I quickly realized that I was really good at process improvement. I was able to take a process and refine it and make the job more efficient for everyone. The leadership team in my department liked the idea of making procedures and processes more efficient so I ended up doing more tasks.

What Is Lifelong Learning?

Lifelong learning is the term used to describe the ongoing, voluntary, and self-motivated pursuit of knowledge for either personal or professional reasons. It implies a willingness to learn new things at any stage in life and to use that knowledge to improve one's life.

There are many good reasons to pursue lifelong learning. First, it can keep your mind sharp and help you stay current in your field. If you're a professional, staying up to date on the latest research and developments in your field can help you be more successful. Even if you're not working, learning new things can help keep your brain active and prevent cognitive decline.

Second, lifelong learning can help you make better decisions. The more knowledge you have, the better equipped you are to make informed decisions about your life, your career, and your future.

Third, lifelong learning can improve your quality of life. Studies have shown that people who engage in lifelong learning are more likely to be satisfied with their lives and have a higher sense of well-being. They're also more likely to be physically active and have a healthier lifestyle overall.

Finally, lifelong learning can simply be enjoyable. It's a chance to explore new topics, expand your horizons, and meet new people. Learning can be a fun and rewarding experience in itself, regardless of any other benefits it may bring.

There are many ways to pursue lifelong learning. You can take classes at a local college or university, participate in online learning opportunities, or simply read books and articles on topics that interest you. There are no limits to what you can learn, so let your curiosity be your guide.

Whatever your reasons for pursuing lifelong learning, remember that it's never too late to start. Learning is a lifelong journey, so jump in and enjoy the ride.

Staying Up to Date on Industry Trends

The best way to stay up to date on industry trends is to read industry-specific news sources and blogs. This will help you to learn about new products, services, and developments in your industry. Additionally, attending industry conferences and networking events is a great way to stay abreast of current trends.

Leadership Trends

Many leadership trends have emerged in recent years. Some of the most popular include servant leadership, authentic leadership, and collaborative leadership. These styles of leadership emphasize different aspects of the leader-follower relationship, but all share a common goal of creating a more effective and productive team.

Leadership Approaches

A *servant leader* is someone who leads by example and puts the needs of others first. A servant leader is someone who is not afraid to get their hands dirty and is always looking for ways to help others. A servant leader is someone who is not afraid to speak up and is always looking for ways to make a difference. A servant leader is someone who is always looking for ways to improve and is never satisfied with the status quo. A servant leader is someone who is always looking for ways to build relationships and is always looking for ways to make a positive impact on those around them.

I was raised on a small farm in Virginia with four brothers and three sisters. Everyone was taught to work hard, earn your own way, and help others along the way. With eight kids and both parents working on the farm, we didn't have a lot of money, but we never went to bed hungry. My parents would barter and trade with workers to help them out. We didn't have money to give them, but my mom would cook food for all the workers. I really didn't understand what my parents were doing at the time, but as I became an adult, I realized they were teaching us to be leaders and understand the importance of helping others.

Of course, we were in church every Sunday, never missed Sunday School, and we also had a singing group. My father was a deacon, and my mom was a missionary, and they knew and understood the importance of leadership and serving others. They taught us to help others in the community first and then become leaders within our community, school, and church. I share this story with you to emphasize what servant leadership is all about. As indicated by Robert Greenleaf, servant leadership is a philosophy and set of practices that enrich the lives of individuals, build better organizations, and ultimately create a more just and caring world.

To further explain servant leadership, let's look at each word separately. First, *servant* . . . individuals who have the feeling or need to serve, which naturally turns into leading. Second, leadership . . . this type of leader does not look for worldly possessions. The ultimate goal of a servant leader is to focus on the growth and well-being of others and the communities in which they live. Servant leaders share power and often let others shine first.

The October 26 reading of the little devotional *Daily Word* was titled "Behind the Scenes." It reminded me of the importance of giving back to our communities. The moral of the reading was focused on leadership... when a leader has achieved a great accomplishment and is waiting for praise, that's when you know they are not servant leaders. When serving the Lord, we should not look for recognition. A Christ-first attitude can subdue any jealousy or unhealthy competition.

According to Chris Edmonds' book *The Culture Engine*,[3] there are seven secrets that can lead you to success as a servant leader:

1. Every person has value and deserves civility, trust, and respect.

2. People can accomplish much when inspired by a purpose beyond themselves.

3. Clarify and reinforce the need for service to others.

4. Listen intently and observe closely.

5. Act as selfless mentors.

6. Demonstrate persistence.

7. Lovingly hold themselves and others accountable for their commitments.

I am not a product of my circumstances. I am a product of my decisions.

— Stephen R. Covey

The first step to leadership is servanthood.

— John Maxwell

---

3 Chris Edmonds, *The Culture Engine: A Framework for Driving Results, Inspiring Your Employees, and Transforming Your Workplace* (Hoboken, NJ: Wiley, 2014).

A ***collaborative leader*** emphasizes building strong relationships with employees and being transparent and ethical in decision-making.

Some qualities that are important for a *collaborative leader* are:

- The ability to listen to others and take their input seriously.
- Respect for others' opinions and the ability to work together towards a common goal.
- Flexibility and the ability to adapt to changing circumstances.
- The ability to motivate and inspire others.
- The ability to see the big picture and make decisions that are in the best interest of the team or organization.

A ***transformational leader*** is someone who motivates and inspires others to achieve their best. This type of leader is focused on the future and is constantly looking for ways to improve. They are also great at communicating their vision and motivating others to follow them.

Be curious and invest in yourself by taking the time to learn new things and pursue your interests. This can be done by reading books, taking classes, or simply exploring the world around you. When you do this, you will not only become more knowledgeable and interesting, but you will also gain a greater sense of self-awareness and confidence. So go out there and start learning!

A ***learning leader*** is a person who can inspire others to learn. They can create a learning environment that is conducive to learning and growth. They possess the necessary skills to facilitate learning and help others to reach their potential.

There are five characteristics of a learning leader:

1. Perception and insight

2. Motivation

3. Emotional strength

4. Ability to change the cultural assumptions

5. Ability to create involvement and participation.

After reviewing the five characteristics, it is quite difficult to select one as they are all important. Involvement and participation are important because they stimulate motivation, keep the employees engaged, and also establish trust with the team as they know the leader is on board with them. When there is a lack of structure and no engagement with the team, things can become chaotic and cause disengagement. However, I decided to focus on another characteristic that is also important. In addition to involvement and participation, employees need to know that their leader is someone whom they can go to for guidance. During times of change, employees want to know that they have someone they can trust, someone they respect, as well as someone who can inspire them and share their perception and insight.

In today's organizations, leaders are tasked with handling external pressures in addition to internal environmental issues. Learning leaders today must be able to deal with the visionary changes that are rapidly occurring in the environment. Having the ability to be agile and flexible is almost essential in today's organizations. Change is constant, frequent, and unpredictable. An effective leader must be prepared to address any potential issues that come up and be able to provide or share some insight into the issues from a cultural perspective.

Employees are often attracted to and will follow an inspirational leader, as they are good role models and people believe in their cause. Having this type of leader creates an environment of engagement and the employees will want to improve more, resulting in a productive work environment. In addition, this type of leader can seek advice from others and learn from others, as they are more receptive to their willingness to share some of their insights with them.

Some people do follow leaders for other reasons such as their social influence or their emotional relationships. For example, during our last reorganization, one of our managers related to his female boss as someone who had more authority and made all of the decisions. He struggled slightly when his boss didn't know all the answers for him during the restructuring. However, he was pleased to know that his leader shared some of her weaknesses with the team, which made him feel better about the changes that were going on in the company.

Failing Forward to Success

Remember, one of the three common fears most people have is fear of failure. If you really want to be successful, though, you have to get used to making mistakes. You have to learn to "fail forward"— you can use all your experiences to build toward success.

For me, the fear of failure popped up several times in life. Most recently was when I was diagnosed with breast cancer. I didn't have the fear of having cancer, but I had the fear of what would happen next. You see, my company was downsizing at the same time as my diagnosis and treatment. So, I opted for early retirement to focus on my health.

Having worked for a company for almost 30 years, I had to figure out how I was going to support myself and my family. I wanted to start a coaching and training business, but I didn't think I was good enough, I didn't have my head in the game of life. So, I had to pull myself out of that space of negative thinking and focus on how I could help people. If you are a person sitting on the sidelines of life, here are three things that helped me overcome the fear of failure, rejection, and thinking I wasn't good enough.

The first thing that helped me push through the fears was developing confidence in myself and believing that I could be a good coach and trainer. Second, I had to change my mindset. I began surrounding myself with other coaches, speakers, and trainers, which allowed me to build new connections and get "unstuck." Planning my schedule intentionally was very helpful as it allowed me to make progress each day. Finally, I had to stop comparing myself to others. Yes, you will have someone who is a better coach, a better speaker, or a better leader, however, no one will coach, speak, or lead the way you do. Remember that done is better than perfect so stop waiting for the right time to get started and Get in the Game!

Dr. Linda's Kernels of Wisdom

So, are you ready to take the leap and invest in yourself?

Write down three things that you will do to invest in YOU and make CHANGE happen for you!

Investment #1

_____

_____

_____

_____

_____

_____

Investment #2

_____

_____

_____

_____

_____

_____

Investment #3

_____

_____

_____

_____

_____

_____

Chapter 7

Be an Inclusive Leader: The Importance of Having a Diverse Culture

A recent study by Gallup[4] indicates that US-based companies are losing $350 billion per year due to disengaged employees. Research has also shown that culture has an effect on the formulation of organizational strategy as well as on overall company performance. When there is a lack of diversity and inclusion, employees become disengaged. Building an inclusive and diverse culture in the workplace creates a healthy work environment and helps to build relationships. To remain competitive and compliant, companies must focus on their culture and the ability of their employees to effectively collaborate and partner with one another.

An organization's culture is its internal environment; it incorporates the values, beliefs, and strategies that all employees share. An organization's culture affects employees' performance, behavior, and overall engagement in the workplace. If an employee

---

4 Jim Harter, "U.S. Employee Engagement Slump Continues," Gallup Workplace, April 25, 2022, https://www.gallup.com/workplace/391922/employee-engagement-slump-continues.aspx.

is not engaged in their work, then they are not satisfied with some aspect of the work environment.

I can remember an experience when I was responsible for creating a business continuity plan for a contact center at a former job. The idea was to set up remote workstations at the home of employees. This would be beneficial for natural disasters and backup for any changes that might impact the contact center. This change was immediately accepted so we established a pilot program to ensure all systems would work. The staff loved the idea and they immediately engaged in the process. After some time of process improvement and showing leadership that there was no negative impact on productivity and there was an increase in employee engagement, the program was approved to be a part of the long-term strategy.

When you provide flexibility in your work schedule for employees, it is a game changer, and it helps with work-family balance.

Creating and maintaining a strong culture can be a challenging task. Corporate leadership must provide consistency by integrating many diverse elements into a set of beliefs, values, assumptions, and behaviors. The term *corporate culture* can be confusing to employees within an organization, but basically, it is the pattern of basic assumptions, values, norms, and behaviors shared by all members of the organization. The senior leadership team is responsible for sharing these patterns with the rest of the company, so everyone has the same level of understanding regarding the everyday life of the organization. Although sharing information is critical and should be a best practice within the organization, it's not always the norm in some organizations. From the top down, leadership must make this a priority, though, if they want their employees to have high engagement. The more leadership can make employees feel valued, the more those employees will internalize the company culture.

Inclusion has three indicators:

1. The degree of influence employees have over decisions that affect them at work.

2. The degree to which employees are kept well-informed about the company's business strategies and goals.

3. The likelihood that employees will keep their jobs.

Being inclusive means that the organization values all employees, and everyone has the opportunity to develop and grow their skills, talents, and capabilities. An inclusive organization means that the employees are engaged, supported, and connected.

Every day, managers must be able to motivate their employees. Managers should be able to determine when their employees are engaged in their work and when they are not engaged or are not productive. Managers must also remember that each employee is different; therefore, what motivates one person may not motivate someone else.

Employee ownership can be motivating. Some opportunities companies can offer their employees include stock option plans, restricted stock plans, employee stock ownership plans (ESOP), and 401(k) plans. Ownership allows employees to understand the company's strategy as well as see the value of being more cost-effective when it comes to budget time. Although providing stock ownership in the company is a good way to motivate employees, it isn't the best alternative for employee engagement because there is no guarantee as to how long the employee will be with the company. Stock ownership and compensation are good short-term motivators, but keep in mind that they have no long-term effects.

Thirty years ago, employees who worked in the public sector placed a greater value on job security. Since that time, employee behavior has changed slightly, and the focus has shifted more to salary and benefits. Most recently, studies have shown that employees feel valued when managers take the time to show them personalized appreciation for a job well done. Employees want to know that someone cares about them. They want to be able to trust their leaders, and they also want to know that the work they do brings value to the organization.

Keeping high-performing employees motivated and engaged requires the same amount of energy as motivating an employee who has an average performance. Managers have to determine what motivates their staff. Each employee has a different way that he or she would like to be recognized. Most employees have three goals in the workplace:

1. To be treated fairly and with respect for equal pay, equal benefits, and job security.

2. To have a sense of accomplishment.

3. To have good partnerships with colleagues.

Unfortunately, some managers tend to assume that providing additional compensation to employees will make them happy and productive. Monetary incentives may consist of awards, additional pay, bonuses, or gift cards. Although employees may be grateful for receiving these incentives for a job well done, they are not completely satisfied or happy. Employees want to be respected by their coworkers and leaders, they want to be treated as adults, and they want to know that their job is not at risk. Managers and business owners who take the time to stop by an employee's work area to see how they are doing or just say hello will have a productive and engaged staff.

As a business owner, I often find myself forgetting about the importance of taking time with staff. Most recently, I reminded myself of this very thing. It was a busy Friday, and everyone was working hard. Although Friday was payday, I decided to buy ice cream for the staff. Everyone was excited to have ice cream but they were more excited to know that I was thinking of them. It only takes a few minutes to show kindness to others, and the impact of this kindness will go a long way.

Diversity Training

These days it's wise to invest in diversity training for your employees. A diversity, equity, and inclusion training program describes the concept of unconscious bias, identifies how these biases can infect critical management decisions in the employee life cycle, help individuals to identify early childhood experiences that may inform the assumptions and biases they hold, provide a description of micro-inequities and the impact on diverse employees, identify individual behaviors that can create or erode inclusion, and implement actions for managing one's biases and behaviors. Diversity training also reiterates the importance of building and maintaining trust, managing expectations and styles when dealing with cross-cultural issues, and recognizing and responding to work style differences. Providing robust diversity training helps employees understand the importance of how diverse interpretations and predictive models lead to more accurate predictions, how multiple perspectives improve problem-solving, and how a diversely equipped group, when managed correctly, can be more productive than a homogeneously equipped group.

It is important to remember that as a neurodiverse society, we all learn differently, and we need to ensure that there is a level of awareness about our differences. Neurodiversity refers to a concept that embraces a range of neurological differences in individuals. It recognizes that people have diverse brain wiring and that these differences should be respected and valued. Neurodivergent individuals may have conditions such as autism, ADHD, dyslexia, Tourette's syndrome, or other cognitive differences. The neurodiversity movement promotes the view that neurological differences should be accepted and accommodated and not viewed as disorders or disabilities that need to be cured or fixed. In addition, participants typically can take a self-assessment during the training to determine their strengths and areas for development within inclusion and diversity.

Another area of focus in diversity, equity, and inclusion training is stereotyping. Stereotyping refers to assuming others have certain characteristics or attitudes simply because they belong to a certain group or category. Although someone might work for a large company, there are still areas within the business that have stereotyping issues. These might be based on physical appearance and lack of departmental fit. Ethnic groups, too, tend to see themselves in stereotypical ways. This is more common with women and minorities. Self-stereotyping varies depending on the identity of the gender or race, and it depends upon what a person thinks of himself or herself. When employees stereotype themselves, it tends to impact their work attitude and performance. In most cases, this will also lead to demotivation in the workplace. A manager who is attentive and notices this type of behavior can take the necessary steps to interrupt and change this pattern. Having this type of leader in the organization is critical. An effective leader should be someone who can identify an employee's performance without causing disruption, someone who can lead the organization, drive change, and inspire the team. It is also very important to have a leader who can relate well to cultural differences and adapt to a changing environment.

The importance of diversity, equity, and inclusion in the workplace is to ensure that everyone understands how to address differences because these have an impact on how employees perform and interact in the workplace. It's also making sure that everyone has an awareness of contrasting values and sensitivities, thus eliminating and reducing obstacles that prevent others from being more inclusive and fully engaged. It is very important to demonstrate respect and fairness in the workplace with clients, employees, and stakeholders.

Employee Engagement

Employee engagement is all about the level of involvement, enthusiasm, and commitment each employee brings to the table. When employees know their purpose and have a strong connection to their work, they are willing to put in extra effort and time to achieve their goals. Engaged employees are typically more productive, more satisfied with their jobs, and less likely to leave their organization. Strategies to increase employee engagement include creating a positive work environment, providing opportunities for development and growth, recognizing and rewarding employee contributions, and fostering open communication and collaboration.

Engaged Employees Are Productive Employees

If managers, supervisors, and other leaders in the company are not keeping their employees motivated and engaged, those employees will eventually leave.

Four ways to determine if an employee is disengaged:

1. The employee is just going through the motions and not giving 100 percent effort.

2. The employee does not show an interest in establishing relationships with colleagues.

3. The employee is not striving for excellence; they are just satisfied with being OK.

4. When communicating virtually, the employee does not show an interest in the meetings.

Four ways to keep your employees engaged

1. Get to know your employees on a personal level and let them know that you care.

2. Provide your employees with developmental opportunities.

3. Keep your employees informed about the company. Let them know they are a part of the company's success.

4. Recognize the team and the individual contributors for their hard work and the success they have achieved.

Your employees are your most valuable resource. Make sure you build a healthy culture that affirms diversity and inclusion and focuses on a high level of employee engagement and you'll be on your way to realizing a happier workplace and a more profitable business!

Dr. Linda's Kernels of Wisdom

1. Take a few moments and answer these three questions: What are you doing to connect with your teams?

_____

_____

_____

_____

_____

_____

_____

_____

_____

_____

2. What steps are you taking to ensure you are promoting your staff based on their capabilities and not because they look like you?

_____

_____

_____

_____

_____

_____

_____

_____

_____

_____

3. Think of a time when someone at work needed empathy. What did you do or what could you have done differently?

_____

_____

_____

_____

_____

_____

_____

_____

_____

_____

CHAPTER 8

Be an Engaged Leader: Don't Be That Crappy Boss!

Having good leadership skills is critical when it comes to maintaining and nurturing today's workforce. According to a December 2021 Gallup study, quality leadership is viewed as being a top priority by **48 percent of leaders** in their current organizations. One of the top challenges for CEOs is developing the next generation of high-quality leaders. In addition, the Gallup study revealed that 63 percent of millennials do not believe their companies and managers are fully preparing them for leadership. Fifty-seven percent of the workforce leave their jobs because their boss is a crappy leader!

We all know that 25 percent of businesses fail in the first year. By the second year, 50 percent of all businesses fail, and, of course, by the fifth year, more than 75 percent of new businesses are closed. Why are businesses failing? Well, it's due to poor leadership.

Being a good leader is more than having a fancy title; it's more than having a big office on the 18th floor, and it is definitely more than making $500,000 a year. *Leadership is about the ability to connect and influence others.*

Most people look at leadership as a position of power. However, having the power to make decisions or being the boss does not make someone a leader. Being a good leader requires a lot of work. A good leader is someone who can influence others, is good at building relationships with others, develops their team, and is respected by others.

Good Leaders Are Good Listeners

The ability to listen to others is a key leadership skill. It doesn't matter if you're a farmer, a business owner, or the manager of a team in a corporate environment, learning to listen well is vital.

- Listening builds relationships.
- Listening increases knowledge.
- Listening generates ideas.
- Listening builds loyalty.
- Listening is a great way to help others.

There are so many listening lessons that I learned on the farm. The listening lesson that stuck with me came from my mother. She always talked to us about making sure that whatever you do in life, make sure you are the best at doing it and give it your all. She taught us that no matter what type of job we had, we should make sure that we gave 110 percent to it. You may not think that anyone is noticing your good work, but be aware that someone is paying attention.

Think about the bosses you've had in your life. When you reflect on the "bad" ones, what qualities come to mind? I guess that they didn't listen well, their employees didn't feel heard or didn't feel that their opinions were valued. In my 30-plus years of working in the corporate space, I have come across a few leaders who were not effective in their leadership roles.

One example of this is when my manager started the role, this person didn't understand how to lead a large team. They came in with their thoughts about what the team should be doing without taking the time to understand and learn what the team's role and responsibilities were before making changes. This leader was not very good at listening to others. Yes, they did take time to have a feedback session, however, the feedback shared was dismissed. This, of course, made me and the team feel like our feedback was not valued and that our voices were not being heard. It was also interesting to see that this leader would bring in senior leadership to show off the good work of the team and would often ask the team to share our experiences in the workplace. Unfortunately, this leader didn't see the value in what the team was doing and eventually began discussing the possibility of outsourcing the department. We all know the meaning of "right-sizing" in the corporate space. Once those words surfaced, everyone on the team became concerned and began to lose trust in this leader. When you cannot trust your leader, then you start to look for other work options and this, of course, is not good for the organization.

Listening is an essential skill that plays a vital role in our personal and professional lives. It is the ability to receive, interpret, and comprehend what is being communicated through verbal and nonverbal cues.

Here are some reasons why listening is important.

- Building relationships: Good listening skills help build better relationships. Whether you are with a work colleague or a family member, attentive listening shows that you care about the person and their thoughts and feelings.
- Learning: Listening is a primary source of learning. By actively listening, we gain knowledge and insights that we might otherwise miss. We can learn from colleagues, mentors, family members, and friends.

- Resolving conflicts: Conflicts are a natural part of any relationship, but they can be resolved more effectively if we are good listeners. Listening to the other person's viewpoint, understanding their perspective, and finding common ground can lead to a mutually beneficial resolution.
- Increasing productivity: Good listening leads to improved productivity at work. Employees who listen actively are better able to follow instructions, understand the goals and objectives of the company, and perform their tasks efficiently.
- Empathizing: Listening allows us to empathize with others, understand their emotions, and support them in their time of need. It helps us connect with others on a deeper level, forming stronger and more meaningful relationships.

In conclusion, listening is a critical skill that we need in every aspect of our lives. It is the foundation of effective communication, and it helps us build meaningful relationships, learn, resolve conflicts, increase productivity, and empathize with others. By practicing active listening, we can improve our personal and professional lives.

Don't be that boss who doesn't listen to his/her staff. Some of the common barriers to listening include:

- Lack of focus
- Mental fatigue
- Self-absorption
- Stereotyping
- Overvaluing talking

What Makes an Engaging Boss?

Engaging bosses inspire their teams to work toward a common goal while creating a positive work environment. They lead by example, listen to their team members, and provide ongoing support and guidance. Engaging bosses are effective communicators who are accessible to their team members, and they embrace change and encourage innovation.

One of the most crucial traits of engaging bosses is their ability to build strong relationships with their team members. They make an effort to get to know each person on their team, understand their strengths and weaknesses, and create opportunities for growth and development. Engaging bosses provide regular feedback, both positive and constructive, to help their team members improve their performance and reach their full potential.

Another key attribute of engaging bosses is their ability to inspire and motivate their team members. They communicate a clear vision and purpose, and they help their team members understand how their contributions fit into the big picture. Engaging leaders recognize team members' achievements and celebrate their successes, which boosts morale and reinforces a sense of teamwork.

Engaging bosses are always learning and growing. They seek out feedback from their team members, colleagues, and mentors, and they continually strive to improve their leadership skills. Engaging leaders are open-minded, adaptable, and willing to try new things, which encourages their team members to do the same.

Finally, engaging bosses are those who create a positive work environment, build strong relationships, inspire and motivate their team members, and constantly learn and grow. These leaders empower their team members to achieve their goals and contribute to the overall success of the organization.

So, in addition to being good listeners, what other qualities make a good leader? Here are six key traits:

1. They effectively communicate with others.

2. They are transparent and trustworthy.

3. They make decisions based on the productivity of the business.

4. They hold themselves accountable.

5. They inspire and influence others.

6. They can overcome challenges and drive change.

These six traits apply whether the leader is a CEO of a corporation, a leader of a team, or the leader of their own startup.

Ten Ways to Identify a Crappy Boss

You know you have a crappy boss when:

1. The boss is always late for work.

2. The boss doesn't know how to create a performance plan.

3. They don't know the basics of their job.

4. They are jealous of your progress.

5. They take credit for your work.

6. They micromanage you but don't hold themselves accountable.

7. They don't provide feedback.

8. They have no idea of the work schedule or how to manage a team.

9. They have favorites on the team.

10. They ask you to work on holidays and weekends.

Don't Be That Boss!

Susan, one of the vice presidents of a large organization, was very optimistic when it came to opportunities she was involved in, and she was very self-driven. Unfortunately, her behavior often came across to her team as negative. She had a high level of self-confidence, which was admirable; however, she didn't seem to be able to effectively communicate with her team.

Another example is when one of my previous employers hired a manager to lead four departments. Of course, the manager didn't have experience managing a sales department, but he had managed teams in the past. But this manager had no idea how to connect and work with or develop others. He was always late, which looked bad to his employees. He also didn't understand how to generate sales for the department. When a manager has to ask his employees how to do his job, you know that the manager isn't qualified for the job.

You Can Be an Engaging Leader

The ability to influence others is an important quality of relationship management. Leaders can influence others and build powerful networks within and outside their organization or network. During my time in corporate, one of my direct reports did an excellent job in building relationships to gain buy-in and support when working on his business plans. He made every attempt to align positive alliances with others to gain cooperation, overcome obstacles, and make progress on business objectives. The most important step he would take was to lead others through an influence approach. He also recognized the importance of others and he always encouraged his team. His ability to establish an alignment of interests with the group allowed me, as the leader, to set the foundation of trust for the department

Dr. Linda's Kernels of Wisdom

Now that you know what it takes to be an engaging leader, take a few moments and answer these three questions:

1. Make a list of the bad habits that you are currently doing and want to change when it comes to leading others:

_____

_____

_____

_____

_____

_____

2. Now, make a list of actions you will take to improve how you lead others and when you will take them:

_____

_____

_____

_____

_____

_____

3. Finally, take a few moments to write down how you plan to measure your results or demonstrate how your efforts will make a positive impact on others:

_____

_____

_____

_____

_____

_____

If you follow these principles, you can avoid being a crappy boss. Working on your leadership skills will make you the most sought-out leader in your industry. If you are struggling with what skills to focus on first, start by taking a few leadership assessments such as the Maxwell DISC assessment, Emotional Intelligence skills assessment, and MBTI, and seek out a leadership coach.

CHAPTER 9

Be in Your Own Power: Know Your Boundaries and Live Life Intentionally

Being in your power means understanding and being comfortable with your abilities and limitations. It's about having a sense of self-awareness and knowing when to assert yourself and when to back down. Setting and enforcing boundaries is an important part of being in your power. My mentor, John C. Maxwell, says, "To be significant, all you have to do is make a difference with others wherever you are, with whatever you have, day by day."

I work hard to ensure that I am living my best life intentionally every day. To live life intentionally, I need to make a difference in someone's life by doing something that makes a difference, especially at a time that will make a difference for others. When I started my coaching business, my primary goal was to make a difference in the world. My goal was and still is to help women learn how to start their own business in real estate, coaching, or whatever their desire is. The goal is to help others just start. Often we hesitate to start a project or business because we are not 100 percent confident in ourselves. You have to trust in your power, know your purpose, and know your why before you can help others. So, let's start with knowing your why!

The Importance of Knowing Your Why

So, what is your why? What gets you out of bed every morning? What keeps you up at night? Is it paying off debt, saving for your child's college, paying off your mortgage, or creating a family legacy? For me, my why was saving for my daughter's college expenses and then creating a family legacy. You see, when I went to college, I didn't have a lot of money and my parents couldn't afford to pay for college, so I wanted to make sure my daughter was in a better situation than I was. I also wanted to make sure that I could leave a family legacy for my daughter so that she would be able to take care of herself later in life. Being a country girl, we didn't grow up having these types of conversations. Yes, we saved our money, but we didn't have enough money to save for college or any large items. Although we didn't have much, my parents always made sure that we had $5 to put in the church collection plate on Sundays. Today, $5 doesn't seem like a lot of money but back then it was a lot. I always wondered how my parents could find the money for church on Sundays when we were going through tough times during the week. My mom always said, "The Lord will bless you when you bless others." Fifty years later, the words she said then now make sense to me because that was my mother's why. She always wanted to help others in any way she could, knowing that she would be blessed in the long run.

It is very important to understand your purpose and know what your goals are. When creating your goals, make sure they are specific, measurable, achievable, realistic, and time-bound.

Living intentionally is about being present and mindful in every aspect of your life. It's about choosing how you want to live your life, rather than just going along with the flow. Here are some tips on how to live intentionally:

- Set goals: Identify what you want to achieve in various areas of your life, such as career, health, relationships, and personal growth. Write them down and create a plan on how to achieve them.
- Prioritize: Prioritize your goals and focus on the most important ones. This will help you to avoid wasting time and energy on things that don't matter.
- Be mindful: Be present in the moment and enjoy what you're doing. Pay attention to your surroundings, your thoughts, and your emotions.
- Simplify: Simplify your life by reducing clutter, eliminating unnecessary commitments, and prioritizing self-care.
- Be grateful: Practice gratitude by acknowledging and appreciating the good things in your life, no matter how small they may be.
- Learn continuously: Learning is a lifelong process, so make time to learn new things and acquire new skills.
- Connect with others: Connect with like-minded people who share your values and goals. It helps you to feel supported and provides opportunities for growth and learning.
- Move forward: Take action to achieve your goals, even if it's just a small step. Progress is progress, no matter how small.

By living intentionally, you can create a life that is fulfilling and meaningful. Remember that it's never too late to start living intentionally – you can choose to start right now!

If you are a business owner or entrepreneur, here are eight ways entrepreneurs can set and enforce boundaries:

1. Understand your values: Understand what is important to you and what you stand for. This will help you to identify and set boundaries that align with your values.

2. Communicate your boundaries: Clearly and assertively communicate your boundaries to others, whether it's in your personal or professional life.

3. Be consistent: Consistently enforce your boundaries, if someone crosses them, it's important to address them immediately.

4. Be flexible: Be open to negotiation and compromise, but also be prepared to stand firm when necessary.

5. Learn to say no: Saying no when necessary can help to protect your time and energy, and to prioritize the things that are important to you.

6. Take responsibility: Take responsibility for your actions and decisions, it will help you to be in control of your own life.

7. Seek support: Surround yourself with people who support you and respect your boundaries, and don't be afraid to seek professional help if needed.

8. Reflect on yourself: Take time to reflect on your behavior, thoughts, and emotions. Understand how they affect your boundaries and how you interact with others.

By understanding and enforcing their boundaries, entrepreneurs can be in their own power and take control of their lives, both personally and professionally. It will help them to manage their time, energy, and resources more effectively, and to prioritize what's important for them and their business.

Knowing your value is essential for success in business and life. Here are some tips to help you understand your value:

- Understand your skills and expertise: Take inventory of the skills and expertise that you bring to the table. This will help you to understand your value and how you can contribute to a team or project.

- Communicate your value: Once you understand your value, it's important to communicate it to others. This can be done through a resume, a pitch, or a simple conversation.

- Negotiate effectively: Knowing your value will help you to negotiate effectively for things like a raise, a promotion, or a new project.

- Provide value to others: The best way to demonstrate your value is by providing value to others. Look for ways to contribute to your team, your company, and your clients.

- Stay informed: Stay informed about industry trends and developments, so you can understand how your skills and expertise align with the needs of the market.

- Be open to learning: Be open to learning new skills and expanding your knowledge, this will help you to stay current and increase your value.

- Know your worth: Knowing your worth means understanding the value that you bring to the table and being willing to ask for what you deserve.

Remember, your value is not just about what you can do, but also about who you are as a person, your experience, attitude, and how you can bring new ideas and perspectives to the table.

Saying no can be difficult, especially in a business setting, but it is an important skill to have as a leader and a business owner. Here are some tips to help you say no effectively:

- Be clear and direct: When saying no, it's important to be clear and direct. Use language that is assertive and confident, but also respectful.
- Explain your reasoning: If possible, explain your reasoning behind saying no. This can help the other person understand and accept your decision.
- Suggest alternatives: If you are unable to do what is being asked, suggest alternatives that might work. This shows that you are willing to help, but also sets clear boundaries.
- Stand your ground: If the other person continues to push, it's important to stand your ground and stick to your decision.
- Don't overcommit: Practice saying no when you are offered something that is not a good fit for you or your business. This will help you to avoid overcommitting and will make it easier to say no when it matters.
- Know your priorities: Knowing your priorities will help you to make decisions about what to say yes and what to say no.

It's also important to remember that saying no is not a rejection of the other person or their ideas, it's just a way of setting boundaries and protecting your time and resources.

Dr. Linda's Kernels of Wisdom

What is your why? If you are not sure, just think about what is your greatest desire in life and write that down.

_____

_____

_____

_____

_____

If you are struggling with managing your time, what are three simple things that you can do to stay on task?

1. _____
   _____
   _____
   _____
   _____

2. _____
   _____
   _____
   _____
   _____

3. _____
   _____
   _____
   _____
   _____

List three barriers that get in your way. Write them down so that you can break through those barriers. This will help you focus on your why.

1. _____
   _____

2. _____
   _____

3. _____
   _____

CHAPTER 10

Be Entrepreneurial: Have More Than One Plan B

By failing to prepare, you are preparing to fail.

—Benjamin Franklin

Having more than one plan, also known as having a contingency or backup plan, is an important aspect of entrepreneurship. It means having alternative strategies in place in case the primary plan does not work out as expected. Most entrepreneurs think that because they are the boss they have a lot of time to figure things out. I am here to tell you that in today's competitive environment, that's not the case. As a business owner, you actually have less time. That's because you are the CEO, the administrator, the bookkeeper, the social media manager, the marketing manager, and more! To be an effective entrepreneur, you need to plan your day, create a business plan, and have a backup for the backup plan!

Having multiple plan Bs can help an entrepreneur to be prepared for various scenarios, such as changes in the market, unexpected competitions, or unplanned obstacles and challenges. It also allows an entrepreneur to quickly pivot and adjust their strategy as needed.

For example, an entrepreneur may have a primary plan to sell their product through retail stores but also have a contingency plan to sell it through an online store if the retail stores do not generate enough sales. Similarly, a startup may have a primary plan to sell its services to one target market but also have a contingency plan to sell it to other target markets in case they are not able to penetrate the primary one.

It's also important to note that having a plan B can also help the entrepreneur be more flexible and open-minded and avoid becoming too attached to a single strategy, which can be detrimental.

When I started my coaching business, I wasn't sure of what my plan was going to be except I knew I wanted to make money. I considered becoming ICF (International Coaching Federation) certified but I didn't have what I needed to start the training program, so I changed my plan. I later found a Life Coaching program that was local in my area, so I signed up. I enjoyed the coaching program, met some new friends, and I learned so much from it. I later joined the John Maxwell program because I wanted to learn more about his teachings and how to apply some of his training to my coaching business. Although this program wasn't in my plan, I knew that learning from John Maxwell would be beneficial to the coaching program that I would offer to others.

Two years later, COVID-19 disrupted our lives, and I found myself having to change my plans again. With no face-to-face meetings, there were no in-person coaching sessions, no training, and no networking. I quickly found myself looking for alternatives to operate safely; hence a Plan B was in the making. Plan B turned into Zoom coaching calls and networking meetings.

When life was getting back to some sense of normalcy, however, I realized I needed to create yet another plan. Plan C was focused on expanding my business into other areas such as speaking and doing more leadership training and workshops. During Plan C, I also decided to invest in myself and signed up for a business coaching program called DRIVEN. This program helped me with time management, business plans and processes, and, most importantly, business marketing. During this time, I was able to learn and understand the importance of diversified marketing and social media. I was in this program for one year and it had a huge impact on my business as well as helping me personally.

At the beginning of 2022, Plan D was formed, and I expanded the coaching part of my business to include a Leadership Academy and online training and became a participant in a docuseries, *The Making of an Entrepreneur.* By diversifying and expanding my business, I was able to reach more clients and break into new networks such as podcasts and radio.

In summary, having multiple plans can help entrepreneurs to be more prepared for unexpected events and to be more adaptable to changes in the market, which can increase the chances of success for the business.

Daily Contingency Plans

There were a few times when my dad had planned to work in the tobacco fields for harvesting and he didn't have the additional help that he thought he would. As an entrepreneur, he would hire a few workers to help out in the fields since most of us kids were young or teenagers. Sometimes, the extra workers were not available to help. So, me and my brothers and sisters who were at home would step in and do what was necessary to get the job done. Often, I was responsible for doing what was called stringing the tobacco on a stick. Once the tobacco was on the stick, my oldest sister would help my dad load the tobacco inside the barn for curing. The curing part occurred when the furnace was lit.

When it came to farming, my parents always taught us to be prepared for what might happen. You see, as in the example above, my dad had a Plan B and was prepared when the workers were not available to help. We, the children, were able to get the job done without the extra help and we completed the work promptly. How many times as a business owner or leader have you had to figure out how to get something done in a short time?

Time Management

I often find myself getting too involved in everything around me simply because I want to be known for having an impact on others. Yes, I am in my own power; however, I can get lost because I am doing too much. Have you ever found yourself in this type of situation? When you are a business owner, you sometimes find yourself overcommitting to doing things for others because you do have some flexibility with your time. If you don't manage your time well, you will become frustrated and then you will start limiting yourself.

Twelve Tips on Time Management

1. Create a schedule - Make a schedule for your day and stick to it as much as possible. This will help you prioritize your time and ensure you complete all necessary tasks. Plan out the day or week in advance and stick to the schedule as closely as possible.

2. Prioritize your tasks - Make a list of all your tasks, and then prioritize them based on their level of importance. This will help you to focus on the most critical tasks first.

3. Break down larger tasks into smaller ones - If a task seems too huge to tackle, break it down into smaller steps. This will make it easier to take on the task and manage your time effectively.

4. Avoid multitasking - It can be tempting to try to accomplish multiple tasks at once, but it only leads to decreased productivity and increased stress. Focus on one task at a time and complete it before moving on to the next.

5. Set clear goals - Set achievable goals for yourself and work towards them. This will help keep you focused and motivated while making sure you remain on track. Setting specific, measurable, attainable, relevant, and time-bound (SMART) goals will focus your efforts and allow you to stay on track.

6. Learn to say no - If someone asks you to do something that will take up too much time or prevent you from completing other important tasks, don't be afraid to say no.

7. Eliminate distractions: Identify and eliminate any distractions that may impede progress, such as social media, email, or phone notifications.

8. Take breaks - It's essential to take regular breaks to recharge your energy and clear your mind. This will help you stay focused and maintain productivity.

9. Use technology wisely - There are many apps and tools available to help manage time effectively. Use them wisely to stay on top of your schedule and improve productivity.

10. Delegate tasks - If possible, delegate tasks to others who can help you complete them quickly and efficiently. This will free up your time to focus on more important tasks.

11. Stay organized: Keep the work environment clean and organized, it can help to reduce stress and increase focus.

12. Review your progress regularly - Review your progress regularly to ensure that you are meeting your goals and making the most of your time. This will also help you identify areas for improvement and adjust your strategy accordingly.

By using these strategies, you can increase your productivity, meet deadlines, and achieve your goals more efficiently in a short time.

I'll share an example from my own life that involved making some changes to my daily schedule. The best and most effective change I made was placing all of my tasks and appointments on my calendar. I enter every fifteen minutes of my day from the time I wake up until the time I go to bed. My calendar includes exercise time, checking emails, lunch, meetings, and even cooking time for dinner. If I didn't place everything on my calendar, I would be overwhelmed and would not be able to get everything done. I was good at procrastinating and telling myself I had plenty of time. I was not good at asking myself, "What are the downsides to not getting this done?" When I began answering this question, I realized why my business wasn't moving forward. It was me! I was procrastinating and making excuses when all I needed to do was complete the work.

One of my biggest struggles in creating my plan of action was being distracted by so much going on. Eliminating distractions is an important aspect of time management and can help entrepreneurs to stay focused on their work and get things done more efficiently.

When I purchased my real estate franchise, I was working from home. I was trying to be cost-effective so I thought setting up a home office would work great. Things started well, but quickly turned into chaos. I found myself doing the laundry when I should be making sales calls. I would stop and watch a few minutes of television on the way to get a drink. That quick five-minute stop turned into thirty minutes of watching a program and missing out on getting to five sales calls. After working from home for about two months, I quickly realized that I needed to be in an office space outside of the home. Once I rented office space, I noticed that I had fewer distractions. I also noticed that I was much more focused being in a different environment and I didn't have to worry about getting the laundry done.

Here are a few strategies that may help eliminate distractions:

- Identify the sources of distraction: Understand what is causing the distraction, whether it's social media, email, phone notifications, or something else.
- Turn off notifications: Turn off all nonessential notifications on your phone, computer, and other devices. This can help to reduce the number of interruptions and allow you to focus on your work.
- Use apps and software to block distractions: There are many apps and software available that can help to block distracting websites and apps during specific times of the day.
- Use noise-canceling headphones: Listening to music or white noise can help to block out external noise and improve concentration.
- Create a designated work space: Having a designated work space can help to create a mental boundary between work and leisure, which can help to reduce distractions.
- Set boundaries with friends and family: Let people know when you are working and need to focus and ask them to respect your boundaries.
- Limit multitasking: Multitasking can decrease productivity and increase distractions, it's better to focus on one task at a time.
- Take breaks: Taking regular breaks can help to reduce distractions and increase productivity.

When it comes to identifying and eliminating distractions, it's important to find the right balance; it's also important to be aware of the importance of taking breaks and disconnecting from time to time. It will help to refresh the mind and increase productivity.

Taking Action

Being ready to take action with a sense of urgency is an essential aspect of entrepreneurship, as it allows entrepreneurs to move quickly and capitalize on opportunities as they arise. When I worked in corporate many years ago, taking action or making decisions was not something that was considered with a sense of urgency. Sometimes, it could take months for any type of action to happen once a decision was made. As a business owner, you can and do make decisions much quicker resulting in fast action.

Here are eight ways entrepreneurs can be ready to take action:

1. Stay informed: Stay up to date with the latest industry trends and news. This will help you anticipate changes and opportunities in the market.

2. Be proactive: Don't wait for opportunities to come to you, actively seek out new opportunities and be prepared to act on them.

3. Have a plan: Have a plan in place for how to take action on opportunities. This can include a strategy for implementing new ideas and a budget for resources.

4. Stay flexible: Be willing to adapt and pivot as needed. The ability to change direction quickly is crucial for success in a fast-paced business environment.

5. Build a network: Build a network of contacts, including potential customers, partners, and investors, which can be valuable resources when opportunities arise.

6. Stay organized: Keep your business and personal life organized, it will help you to quickly access the information you need and make decisions faster.

7. Be decisive: Make quick and confident decisions, weigh the pros and cons, and be prepared to live with the consequences.

8. Take calculated risks: Be willing to take risks when opportunities arise, but make sure to evaluate the potential risks and rewards before taking action.

By staying informed, being proactive, having a plan, staying flexible, building a network, staying organized, being decisive, and taking calculated risks, entrepreneurs can be ready to take action and capitalize on opportunities as they arise. Don't be that entrepreneur who creates a plan and takes no action. It's important to stay on top of your plans. Every 90 days, do an inventory of how your plan is working. If things are going well, that's great. If you see that your plan is not working the way you expected it to, then stop and make any necessary adjustments. Your Plan B is only as good as you make it, work it, and monitor it.Top of Form

Dr. Linda's Kernels of Wisdom

Know that it's OK to change your plans. Nothing is permanent and plans are subject to change. What is your Plan B for your business, your life, and your health? Write it here:

_____

_____

_____

_____

_____

_____

_____

_____

Manage your time wisely. There are 24 hours in a day, so don't mess this up!

Write down what your schedule is for this week:

_____

_____

_____

_____

_____

_____

Distractions take up most of your time. What are those distractions? How do you plan to remove these distractions so that you can be successful?

_____

_____

_____

_____

_____

_____

www.ingramcontent.com/pod-product-compliance
Lightning Source LLC
Chambersburg PA
CBHW031903200326
41597CB00012B/528